King of Glory, King of Peace

A festival service celebrating
the Kingship of Christ

compiled by
Christopher Chivers, Andrew Reid and Tim Ruffer

R S ✦ M

THE ROYAL SCHOOL OF CHURCH MUSIC
19 The Close, Salisbury, Wiltshire, SP1 2EB, England
Tel: +44 (0)1722 424848 Fax: +44 (0)1722 424849
Email: press@rscm.com Website: www.rscm.com
Registered charity 312828

King of Glory, King of Peace

RSCM Catalogue Number: RS53
RSCM Music Direct Order Code: S0176
ISBN: 978-0-85402-270-0

Cover design by Anthony Marks
Cover image: Tympanum depicting "the good shepherd". Mosaic, mid 5th century.
Mausoleum of empress Galla Placidia (St. Nazarius and Celsus, c. 440 AD).

Music setting by Donald Thomson and RSCM Press
With thanks to Daniel Soper
Printed in Great Britain by Halstan & Co, Amersham, UK.

CONTENTS

Introduction iv

Outline of the Service vi

Suggested Order of Service for Choral Evensong ix

THE COMING KING 1

THE BIRTH OF A KING 19

THE TEACHING KING 30

PRAISE FOR THE KING 31

THE SHEPHERD KING 37

THE SERVANT KING 68

HIS KINGLY RULE IN US 86

THE KING OF GLORY 100

ADDITIONAL CHORAL RESOURCES 165

Pastoral Introduction

As the RSCM celebrates its ninetieth anniversary so the festival service takes the kingship of Christ as its theme, and articulates this through defining scriptural passages in the Hebrew Bible and New Testament, the poetry of George Herbert, who gives us the title, *King of Glory, King of Peace*, and music across the generations.

This conflation of anniversary celebration and kingship could risk a misplaced sense of triumphalism at different levels. Since Christians have often managed to project earthly patterns of kingship - with their sense of stratified hierarchy and power - onto the reality of a God whose power is made perfect in weakness and whose reign is made manifest as, girded with a towel, Christ kneels on the floor of an upper room to wash the dirt off his friend's feet.

Members of the RSCM the world over have said the Chorister's Prayer across these ninety years:

> Bless, O Lord, us thy servants who minister in thy temple.
> Grant that what we sing with our lips we may believe in our hearts,
> and what we believe in our hearts we may show forth in our lives;
> through Jesus Christ our Lord.

As they've done so they've defined the ministry of musicians as the offering of everything that we have to God because everything that we have is gift to us from God. This self-offering is the Christian take on kingship.

In an age where power continues so often to be abused, where the might of tyranny crushes the daily hopes and aspirations of the Gospel for so many - hopes for freedom and fullness of life - we celebrate then the imperishable hope of our calling as disciples. In celebrating we encourage one another to bring in the reign of God's kingdom 'on earth as it is in heaven'.

To this task, some words of the Auschwitz survivor Elie Wiesel draw striking attention:

> 'Through song we climb to the highest palace. From that palace we can influence the universe and its prisons. Song is Jacob's ladder forgotten on earth by the angels. Sing and we defeat death; sing and we disarm the foe.'

Help us, King of glory, King of peace, who use this celebration resource, so to sing your praises, that our hearts will turn to the oppressed in their misery and our actions will win them liberation.

Chris Chivers
Principal,
Westcott House, Cambridge

Using the book

There are at least two options for all the musical items in this service. With the hymns, there is a choice between traditional hymnody, and worship songs or contemporary hymns. For many situations it is likely that a mixture of old and new will be found most appropriate. We have also provided choral items suitable for full SATB choirs and those with more limited resources. The first anthem in a group of three is the easiest, and the last the most difficult. Equally suitable for Area Festivals performed by hundreds and for smaller local services, *King of Glory, King of Peace* provides invaluable resources for churches of all sizes.

The service is through composed. Should you choose the first musical option, at the end of that item there is guidance for where to pick up the service, missing out the musical items you won't be using.

The book also provides resources so that it may be adapted for use at Choral Evensong, and guidance for using the book under those circumstances can be found on page ix.

Some Area Festivals feature music that *Voice for Life* award winners can sing. We have provided a number of opportunities for this:

> Brother James's Air by Gordon Jacob: bars 38–46
>
> The King of love by Edward Bairstow: bars 82–96
>
> The Lord is my shepherd by Lennox Berkeley: bars 2–12
>
> What wondrous love is this by Philip Moore: bars 36–55
>
> Te Deum by John Ireland: bars 112–121

Additionally, a verse of a hymn could be sung by award winners alone.

A congregational service leaflet can be found on the RSCM website: www.rscmshop.com/s0176.html

Please note that words of the hymns in copyright require a CCLI licence to reproduce in a service leaflet.

Andrew Reid & Tim Ruffer
RSCM

OUTLINE OF THE SERVICE

THE COMING KING

Introit:

Peter Nardone: O sing to the Lord 2
or
Pitoni: Cantate Domino 9
or
arr. William Llewellyn: Joy to the world 12

Greeting 17

Reading: Zechariah 9: 9-10 18

THE BIRTH OF A KING

Hymn

Lo, he comes with clouds descending 20
or
Love divine, all loves excelling 26
or
Into the darkness of this world 28

THE TEACHING KING

Reading: The Elixir, George Herbert 30

PRAISE FOR THE KING

Psalm 145

Responsorial Chant 31
or
Anglican Chant 32
or
Scottish Metrical 34

Reading: 1 Samuel 16 35

THE SHEPHERD KING

Anthem

Jacob: Brother James's Air   38
or
Bairstow: The King of love   46
or
Berkeley: The Lord is my shepherd   59

THE SERVANT KING

Reading: John 13: 1-17   68

Anthem

Philip Moore: What wondrous love is this!   69
or
Richard Shephard: A new commandment   76
or
Duruflé: Ubi Caritas   78

Hymn

This is your coronation   82
or
To mock your reign   84

HIS KINGLY RULE IN US

Reading: Praise (II), George Herbert (from The Temple, 1633)   86

Hymn

Alleluia, sing to Jesus   88
or
Crown him with many crowns   90
or
King of Kings, majesty   94

Address

THE KING OF GLORY

Anthem

Purcell: O God, the King of Glory 100
or
Ireland: Te Deum in F 106
or
Marenzio: O Rex gloriae 123

Presentation of Awards

128

Prayers

using Antiphon, George Herbert (from The Temple, 1633) 128

Anthem

Philip Duffy: A Song of Salvation 130
or
Bairstow: Let all mortal flesh 134
or
Rachmaninoff: The Cherubic Hymn 143

Blessing

153

Recessional Hymn

Rejoice the Lord is King 154
or
You're the word of God the Father 160

ADDITIONAL CHORAL RESOURCES

Preces & Responses by Harry Bramma 166

Magnificat & Nunc dimittis by Grayston Ives 173

Suggested Order of Service for Choral Evensong

Opening Hymn: Love divine, all loves excelling	26
Preces: Bramma	166
Psalm 145 (Anglican chant)	32
Office Hymn: Crown him with many crowns	90
Magnificat: Ives	173
Nunc dimittis: Ives	182
Responses: Bramma	168
Anthem: O God, the King of Glory by Purcell	100
or	
Anthem: Let all mortal flesh keep silence by Bairstow	134
Hymn: Rejoice the Lord is King	154

King of Glory, King of Peace

THE COMING KING

Introit

Peter Nardone: O sing to the Lord (page 2)
> *or*

Pitoni: Cantate Domino (page 9)
> *or*

William Llewellyn: Joy to the world (page 12)

Introit: O sing to the Lord a new song

Words: PSALM 149

Music: PETER NARDONE
(*b.* 1965)

turn to page 17

Introit: Cantate Domino

Words: PSALM 149

Music: GIUSEPPE OTTAVIO PITONI (1657–1743)

Lae - te - tur Is - ra-el in e - o, lae - te - tur, lae -

-te - tur in e - o, qui fe - cit e - um: et

fi - li - ae Si - on, et fi - li - ae

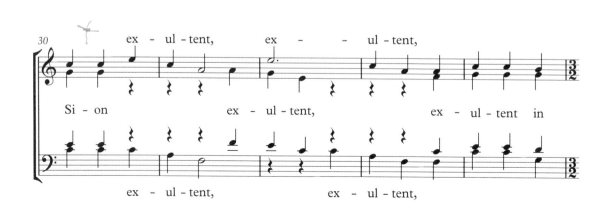

ex - ul -tent, ex - ul -tent,

Si - on ex - ul -tent, ex - ul - tent in

ex - ul -tent, ex - ul -tent,

re - ge su - o, ex - ul - tent, ex -

-ul - tent in re - ge su - o.

Translation: Sing to the Lord a new song:
give praise to him in the assembly of the saints.
Let Israel rejoice in him who made him:
and the daughters of Sion exult in their king.

turn to page 17

Anthem: Joy to the world

Words: ISAAC WATTS
based on PSALM 98

Music: mostly from Holford's *Voce di Melodia* (c.1834)
arranged by WILLIAM LLEWELLYN

continue to next page

Greeting

Christ is the image of the invisible God, the firstborn of all creation; for in him all things were created, things visible and invisible, whether thrones or dominions or rulers or powers - all things have been created through him and for him.

These words from St Paul's letter to the Colossians chapter 1 verses 15 to 16 are pivotal in our understanding of who Christ is for us.

Christ, the King, the word made flesh, makes the invisible God known in human flesh. He becomes one of us and each of us therefore bears this divine image. We are at one with him in the body of Christ which is the Church and subject to Christ's just and gentle, challenging and renewing rule.

This is what it means to be a Christian, to be a citizen of a kingdom on earth as it is in heaven.

From the cradle to the grave and beyond it Christ's kingship is revealed in the glories of humility and vulnerability: humility from the Latin *humus* - earthed; vulnerability from the Latin *vilnius* - wounded. These offer the fundamental characteristics of his rule.

Angels may fanfare his birth but it is poor shepherds who first visit the manger and define his role as one in the tradition of David, the first king, who speaks truth to power from a position of seeming weakness. This weakness is always earthed, rooted in the cost of discipleship because it is none other than that feet-washing love which transforms the world.

As we welcome one another to this place for this service of prayer and praise, we embrace again this way of sacrificial offering and offer the gift of music to God's glory now.

Reading: Zechariah 9: 9-10

> Rejoice greatly, O daughter Zion!
>> Shout aloud, O daughter Jerusalem!
> Lo, your king comes to you;
>> triumphant and victorious is he,
> humble and riding on a donkey,
>> on a colt, the foal of a donkey.
> He will cut off the chariot from Ephraim
>> and the warhorse from Jerusalem;
> and the battle-bow shall be cut off,
>> and he shall command peace to the nations;
> his dominion shall be from sea to sea,
>> and from the River to the ends of the earth.

THE BIRTH OF A KING

Hymn

Lo, he comes with clouds descending (page 20)
or
Love divine, all loves excelling (page 26)
or
Into the darkness of this world (page 28)

Hymn: Lo, he comes with clouds descending

HELMSLEY

8 7 8 7 4 7 extended

1   Lo, he comes with clouds descending,
    once for favoured sinners slain;
thousand thousand saints attending
    swell the triumph of his train:
      Alleluia!
    God appears on earth to reign.

2   Every eye shall now behold him
    robed in dreadful majesty;
those who set at naught and sold him,
    pierced and nailed him to the tree,
      deeply wailing,
    shall the true Messiah see.

3   Those dear tokens of his passion
    still his dazzling body bears;
cause of endless exultation
    to his ransomed worshippers:
      with what rapture
    gaze we on those glorious scars!

Please turn over for last verse harmonisation and descant

4   Yea, Amen, let all adore thee,
    high on thine eternal throne;
Saviour, take the power and glory,
    claim the kingdom for thine own:
      O come quickly!
    Alleluia! Come, Lord, come!

CHARLES WESLEY (1707–1788),
MARTIN MADAN (1726–1790),
and JOHN CENNICK (1718–1755)

The fifth line of each verse is sung three times.

Music: Melody adapted from John Wesley's
Select Hymns with Tunes Annext, 1765
Last verse harmonisation and descant by MARTIN HOW (*b.* 1931)

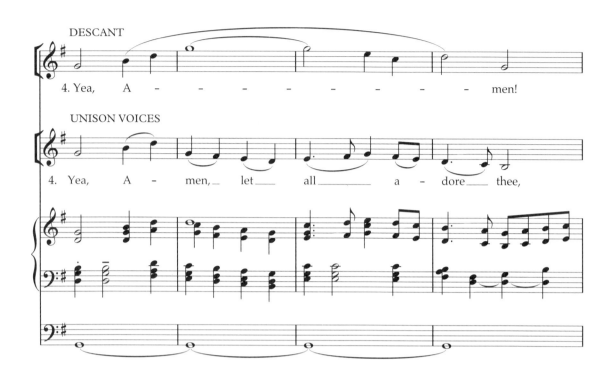

Sa - viour,__ take__ the__ power__ and__ glo - ry,

Sa - viour,__ take__ the__ power__ and__ glo - ry,

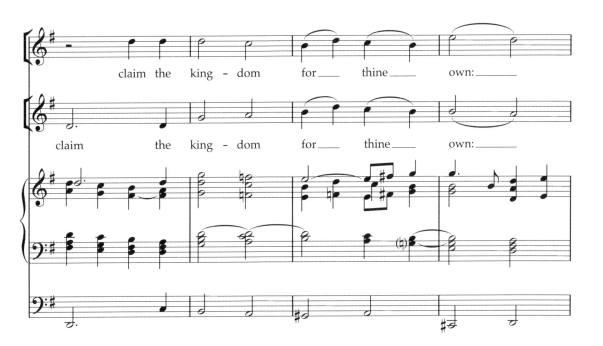

claim the king - dom for__ thine__ own:_____

claim the king - dom for__ thine__ own:_____

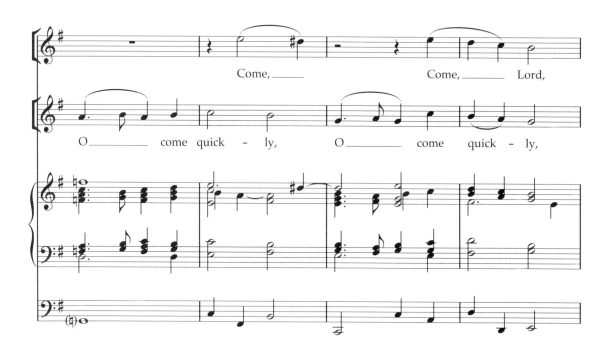

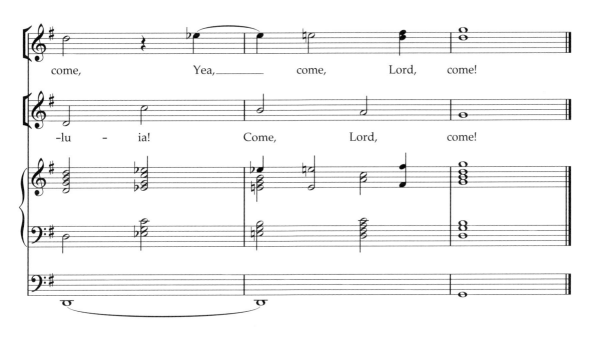

come, Yea,_____ come, Lord, come!

-lu - ia! Come, Lord, come!

turn to page 30

Hymn: Love divine, all loves excelling

BLAENWERN

8 7 8 7 D

Music: WILLIAM PENFRO ROWLANDS (1860–1937)

1 Love divine, all loves excelling,
       joy of heaven to earth come down,
   fix in us thy humble dwelling,
       all thy faithful mercies crown.
   Jesu, thou art all compassion,
       pure, unbounded love thou art;
   visit us with thy salvation,
       enter every trembling heart.

2 Come, almighty to deliver,
       let us all thy grace receive;
   suddenly return, and never,
       never more thy temples leave.
   Thee we would be always blessing,
       serve thee as thy hosts above;
   pray, and praise thee, without ceasing,
       glory in thy perfect love.

3 Finish then thy new creation:
       pure and spotless let us be;
   let us see thy great salvation
       perfectly restored in thee:
   Changed from glory into glory
       till in heaven we take our place,
   till we cast our crowns before thee,
       lost in wonder, love, and praise!

CHARLES WESLEY (1707–1788)

For Choral Evensong, turn to page 166

turn to page 30

Hymn: Into the darkness

Into the dark - ness once a - gain,__ O come, Lord Je - sus, come.
un - til in you__ our hearts u - nite,__ O come, Lord Je - sus, come.
Now let your love__ be born in us__ O come, Lord Je - sus, come.

Refrain

(1,2) Come with your love__ to make us whole,__ come with your light
(3) Come in your glo - ry take__ your place,__ Je - sus the Name

to lead__ us on,_____ dri-ving the dark - ness far from our souls:
a - bove__ all names,__ we long to see__ you face__ to face:

final verse

O come, Lord Je - sus, come.__
O come, Lord Je - sus, come.__

Words and Music: MAGGI DAWN (b. 1959)

turn to next page

THE TEACHING KING

Reading: The Elixir

Teach me, my God and King,
   In all things Thee to see,
And what I do in anything
   To do it as for Thee.

Not rudely, as a beast,
   To run into an action;
But still to make Thee prepossest,
   And give it his perfection.

A man that looks on glass,
   On it may stay his eye;
Or if he pleaseth, through it pass,
   And then the heav'n espy.

All may of Thee partake:
   Nothing can be so mean,
Which with his tincture—"for Thy sake"—
   Will not grow bright and clean.

A servant with this clause
   Makes drudgery divine:
Who sweeps a room as for Thy laws,
   Makes that and th' action fine.

This is the famous stone
   That turneth all to gold;
For that which God doth touch and own
   Cannot for less be told.

GEORGE HERBERT (*from* THE TEMPLE, 1633)

PRAISE FOR THE KING

Psalm 145 (Responsorial) (see below)
or
Psalm 145 (Anglican Chant) (page 32)
or
Psalm 145 (Metrical) (page 34)

Psalm 145 (Responsorial)

1   I will give you glory, O / God my / king,
    I will bless your / name for / ever.
    I will bless you day / after / day
    and praise your / name for / ever.

2   You are great, Lord, highly / to be / praised,
    your greatness can / not be / measured.
    Age to age shall pro- / claim your / works,
    shall declare your / mighty / deeds.

3   All your creatures shall thank / you, O / Lord,
    and your friends shall re- / peat their / blessing.
    They shall speak of the glory / of your / reign
    and declare your / might, O / God.

4   To make known to all your / mighty / deeds
    and the glorious splendour / of your / reign,
    Yours is an ever- / lasting / Kingdom;
    your rule lasts from / age to / age.

PSALM 145 (144): 1–4, 10–13
The Grail Psalter

Music: ANDREW REID

turn to page 35

Psalm 145 (Anglican chant)

THOMAS ATTWOOD WALMISLEY

f 1 I will magnify thee O / God my / King:
        And I will praise thy / Name for / ever • and / ever.

    2 Every day will I give / thanks • unto / thee:
        And praise thy / Name for / ever • and / ever.

    3 Great is the Lord ★ and marvellous / worthy • to be / praised:
        There / is no / end of • his / greatness.

    4 One generation shall / praise thy / works: ⌣
        unto an- / other ★ • and de- / clare thy / power.

    5 As for me I will be / talking • of thy / worship:
        Thy glory thy / praise and / wondrous / works;

    6 So that men shall speak of the might of thy / marvel-lous / acts:
        And I will / also / tell of • thy / greatness.

2nd Part
† 7 The memorial of thine abundant / kindness • shall be / shewed:
        And / men shall / sing of • thy / righteousness.

mp 8 The Lord is / gracious • and / merciful:
        Long-suffering / and of / great ---- / goodness.

    9 The Lord is / loving • unto / every man:
        And his mercy is / over / all his / works.

Thomas Attwood Walmisley

mf   10 All thy works / praise thee • O / Lord:
        And thy / saints give / thanks • unto / thee.

     11 They shew the / glory • of thy / kingdom:
        And / talk ---- / of thy / power;

f   12 That thy power, thy glory and mightiness / of thy / kingdom:
        Might be / known ---- / unto / men.

     13 Thy kingdom is an ever- / lasting / kingdom:
        And thy dominion en- / dureth • through- / out all / ages.

        Glory be to the Father ⋆ and / to the / Son:
        And / to the / Holy / Ghost.

        As it was in the beginning ⋆ is now and / ever / shall be:
        World without / end. ⋆ A- / - - / men.

PSALM 145: 1–13
The Book of Common Prayer

For Choral Evensong, turn to page 90   *turn to page 35*

Psalm 145 (Metrical)

WARRINGTON   LM

1 O Lord, thou art my God and King;
    Thee will I magnify and praise:
  I will thee bless, and gladly sing
    Unto thy holy name always.

2 Each day I rise I will thee bless,
    And praise thy name time without end:
  Much to be praised, and great God is;
    His greatness none can comprehend.

3 Race shall thy works praise unto race,
    The mighty acts show done by thee;
  I will speak of the glorious grace
    And honour of thy majesty.

4 Thy wondrous works I will record:
    By men the might shall be extolled
  Of all thy dreadful acts, O Lord:
    And I thy greatness will unfold.

5 They utter shall abundantly
    The memory of thy goodness great;
  And shall sing praises cheerfully,
    Whilst they thy righteousness relate.

The Scottish Psalter (1650)
JOHN CRAIG (1512–1600) *from* PSALM 145

Music: RALPH HARRISON (1748–1810)

continue to next page

Reading: 1 Samuel 16

The Lord said to Samuel, 'How long will you grieve over Saul? I have rejected him from being king over Israel. Fill your horn with oil and set out; I will send you to Jesse the Bethlehemite, for I have provided for myself a king among his sons.' Samuel said, 'How can I go? If Saul hears of it, he will kill me.' And the Lord said, 'Take a heifer with you, and say, "I have come to sacrifice to the Lord." Invite Jesse to the sacrifice, and I will show you what you shall do; and you shall anoint for me the one whom I name to you.' Samuel did what the Lord commanded, and came to Bethlehem. The elders of the city came to meet him trembling, and said, 'Do you come peaceably?' He said, 'Peaceably; I have come to sacrifice to the Lord; sanctify yourselves and come with me to the sacrifice.' And he sanctified Jesse and his sons and invited them to the sacrifice.

When they came, he looked on Eliab and thought, 'Surely the Lord's anointed is now before the Lord.' But the Lord said to Samuel, 'Do not look on his appearance or on the height of his stature, because I have rejected him; for the Lord does not see as mortals see; they look on the outward appearance, but the Lord looks on the heart.' Then Jesse called Abinadab, and made him pass before Samuel. He said, 'Neither has the Lord chosen this one.' Then Jesse made Shammah pass by. And he said, 'Neither has the Lord chosen this one.' Jesse made seven of his sons pass before Samuel, and Samuel said to Jesse, 'The Lord has not chosen any of these.' Samuel said to Jesse, 'Are all your sons here?' And he said, 'There remains yet the youngest, but he is keeping the sheep.' And Samuel said to Jesse, 'Send and bring him; for we will not sit down until he comes here.' He sent and brought him in. Now he was ruddy, and had beautiful eyes, and was handsome. The Lord said, 'Rise and anoint him; for this is the one.' Then Samuel took the horn of oil, and anointed him in the presence of his brothers; and the spirit of the Lord came mightily upon David from that day forward. Samuel then set out and went to Ramah.

Now the spirit of the Lord departed from Saul, and an evil spirit from the Lord tormented him. And Saul's servants said to him, 'See now, an evil spirit from God is tormenting you. Let our lord now command the servants who attend you to look for someone who is skilful in playing the lyre; and when the evil spirit from God is upon you, he will play it, and you will feel better.' So Saul said to his servants, 'Provide for me someone who can play well, and bring him to me.'

One of the young men answered, 'I have seen a son of Jesse the Bethlehemite who is skilful in playing, a man of valour, a warrior, prudent in speech, and a man of good presence; and the Lord is with him.' So Saul sent messengers to Jesse, and said, 'Send me your son David who is with the sheep.' Jesse took a donkey loaded with bread, a skin of wine, and a kid, and sent them by his son David to Saul. And David came to Saul, and entered his service. Saul loved him greatly, and he became his armour-bearer. Saul sent to Jesse, saying, 'Let David remain in my service, for he has found favour in my sight.' And whenever the evil spirit from God came upon Saul, David took the lyre and played it with his hand, and Saul would be relieved and feel better, and the evil spirit would depart from him.

THE SHEPHERD KING

Anthem

Jacob: Brother James's Air (page 38)
> *or*
Bairstow: The King of love my shepherd is (page 46)
> *or*
Berkeley: The Lord is my shepherd (page 59)

Anthem: Brother James's Air

Words: PSALM 23

Music: JAMES LEITH MACBETH BAIN (1860–1925)
arranged by GORDON JACOB (1895–1984)

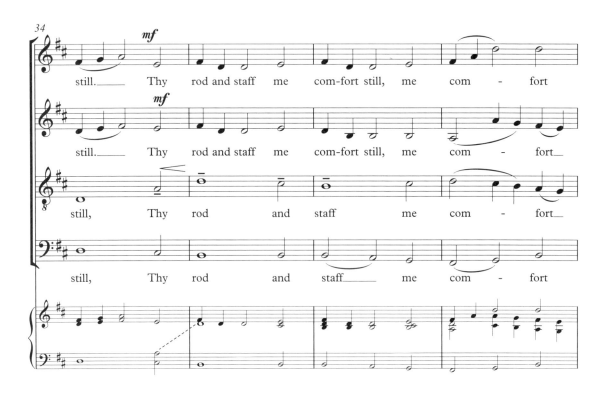

turn to page 68

Anthem: The King of love my shepherd is

Words: HENRY WILLIAMS BAKER (1821–1877)
based on PSALM 23

Music: Traditional Irish hymn melody
arranged by EDWARD C. BAIRSTOW (1874–1946)

* If the notes in small type are played, this Anthem may be sung in unison.
They may also be used when the choir is not able to sing without support from the organ.

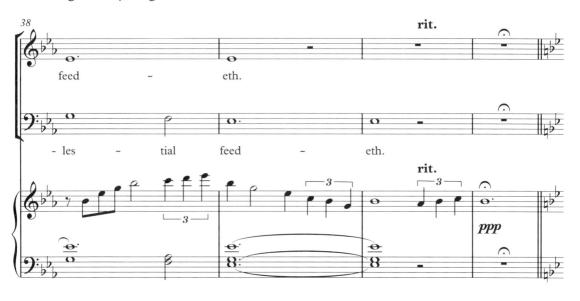

feed - eth.

- les - tial feed - eth.

Più animato, ma maestoso

BASSES *mp*

In__ death's dark

Più animato, ma maestoso

Full Sw. *mp*

Ped.

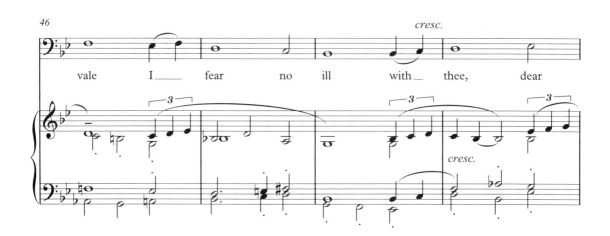

vale I__ fear no ill with_ thee, dear

cresc.

cresc.

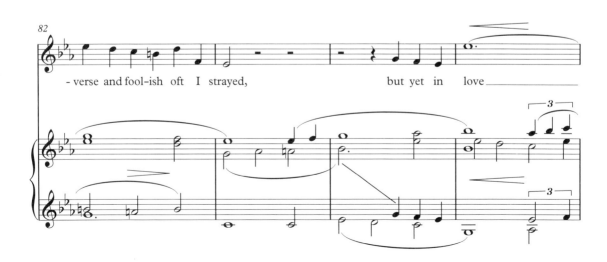

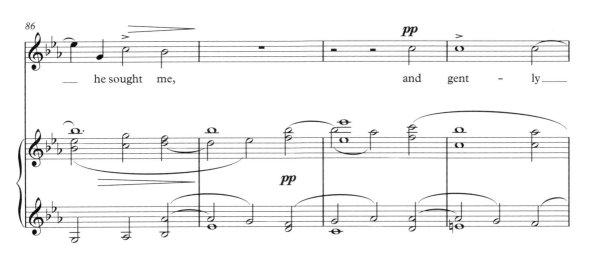

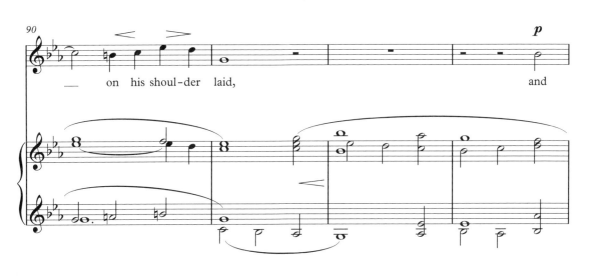

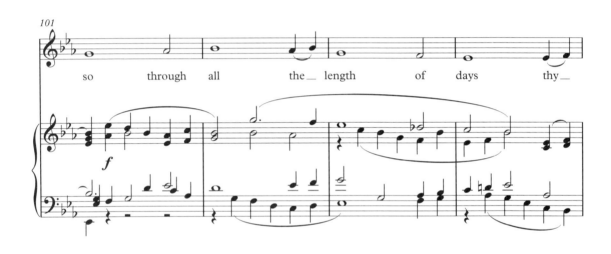

turn to page 68

Anthem: The Lord is my Shepherd

Words: PSALM 23   *Music:* LENNOX BERKELEY
                                                                              (1903–1989)

April 1975

turn to next page

THE SERVANT KING

Reading: John 13: 1–17

Now before the festival of the Passover, Jesus knew that his hour had come to depart from this world and go to the Father. Having loved his own who were in the world, he loved them to the end. The devil had already put it into the heart of Judas son of Simon Iscariot to betray him. And during supper Jesus, knowing that the Father had given all things into his hands, and that he had come from God and was going to God, got up from the table, took off his outer robe, and tied a towel around himself. Then he poured water into a basin and began to wash the disciples' feet and to wipe them with the towel that was tied around him. He came to Simon Peter, who said to him, 'Lord, are you going to wash my feet?' Jesus answered, 'You do not know now what I am doing, but later you will understand.' Peter said to him, 'You will never wash my feet.' Jesus answered, 'Unless I wash you, you have no share with me.' Simon Peter said to him, 'Lord, not my feet only but also my hands and my head!' Jesus said to him, 'One who has bathed does not need to wash, except for the feet, but is entirely clean. And you are clean, though not all of you.' For he knew who was to betray him; for this reason he said, 'Not all of you are clean.'

After he had washed their feet, had put on his robe, and had returned to the table, he said to them, 'Do you know what I have done to you? You call me Teacher and Lord—and you are right, for that is what I am. So if I, your Lord and Teacher, have washed your feet, you also ought to wash one another's feet. For I have set you an example, that you also should do as I have done to you. Very truly, I tell you, servants are not greater than their master, nor are messengers greater than the one who sent them. If you know these things, you are blessed if you do them.'

Anthem

Philip Moore: What wondrous love is this (page 69)
    or
Richard Shephard: A new commandment (page 76)
    or
Duruflé: Ubi Caritas (page 78)

Anthem: What wondrous love

Words: AMERICAN FOLK HYMN *c.* 1835

Music: THE SOUTHERN HARMONY 1835
arranged by PHILIP MOORE

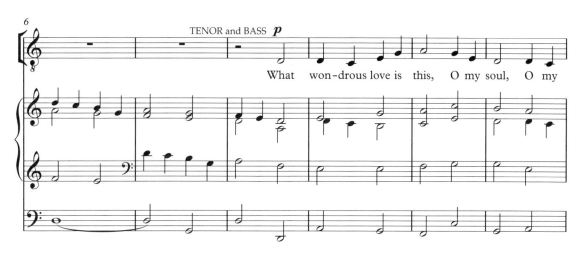

TENOR and BASS

What won-drous love is this, O my soul, O my

soul! What won-drous love is this, O my soul!_____ What won-drous love is

this that caused the Lord of bliss to lay a-side his crown for my soul, for my

soul, to lay a-side his crown for my soul.

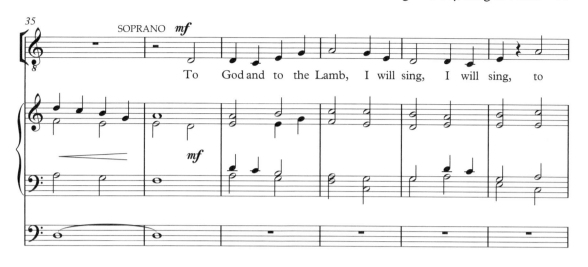

To God and to the Lamb, I will sing, I will sing, to

God and to the Lamb I will sing. To God and to the

Lamb who is the great I AM, while mil-lions join the theme, I will

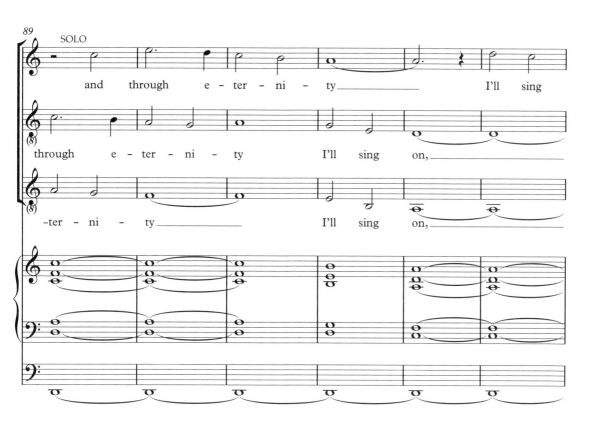

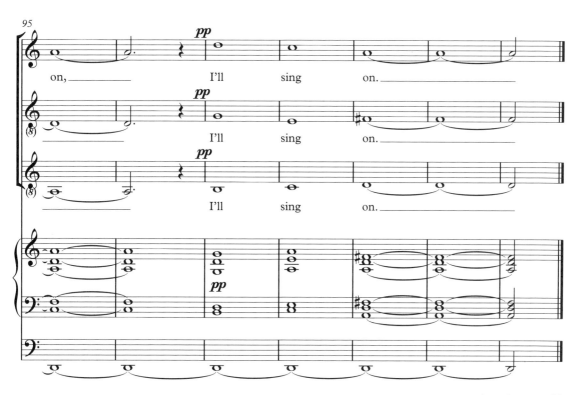

turn to page 82

Anthem: A new commandment

Words: based on JOHN 13. 34–45

Music: RICHARD SHEPHARD

turn to page 82

Anthem: Ubi Caritas

Words: from LIBER USUALIS

Music: MAURICE DURUFLÉ
(1902–1986)

Translation: Where charity and love are, God is there.
Christ's love has gathered us into one. Let us rejoice and be pleased in Him.
Let us fear, and let us love the living God.
And may we love each other with a sincere heart. Amen.

turn to next page

Hymn

This is your coronation (see below)
or
To mock your reign (page 84)

Hymn: This is your coronation

PASSION CHORALE   76 76 D

Music:　Traditional secular meoldy
　　　　in Hans Leo Hassler's *Lustgarten neuer teutscher Gesäng*, 1601
　　　　hamonised by Johann Sebastian Bach (1685–1750)

1   This is your coronation-
        thorns pressed upon your head;
    no bright angelic heralds,
        but angry crowds instead;
    beneath your throne of timber,
        and struggling with the load,
    you go in cruel procession
        on sorrow's royal road;

2   Eternal judge on trial,
        God's law, by law denied;
    love's justice is rejected
        and truth is falsified.
    We who have charged, condemned you
        are sentenced by your love;
    your blood pronounces pardon
        as you are stretched above.

3   High Priest, you are anointed
        with blood upon your face,
    and in this hour appointed
        the offering for our race.
    For weakness interceding;
        for sin, you are the price;
    for us your prayer unceasing,
        O living sacrifice.

SYLVIA G DUNSTAN (1955-1993)

turn to page 86

Hymn: To mock your reign, O dearest Lord

THIRD MODE MELODY   DCM

1 To mock your reign, O dear-est Lord, they made a crown of thorns;
2 In mock ac-claim, O gra-cious Lord, they snatched a pur-ple cloak,
3 A scep-tred reed, O pa-tient Lord, they thrust in-to your hand,

set you with taunts a-long that road from which no one re-turns.
your pas-sion turned, for all they cared, in-to a sol-dier's joke.
and act-ed out their grim cha-rade to its ap-poin-ted end.

They could not know, as we do now, how glo-rious is that crown:
They could not know, as we do now, that, though we me-rit blame,
They could not know, as we do now, though em-pires rise and fall,

that thorns would flower up-on your brow, your sor-rows heal our own.
you will your robe of mer-cy throw a-round our na-ked shame.
your king-dom shall not cease to grow till love em-bra-ces all.

Music: Contributed by THOMAS TALLIS (C. 1505–1585)
to Parker's *The Whole Psalter*

1 To mock your reign, O dearest Lord,
    they made a crown of thorns;
set you with taunts along the road
    from which no one returns.
They could not know, as we do now,
    how glorious is that crown:
that thorns would flower upon your brow,
    your sorrows heal our own.

2 In mock acclaim, O gracious Lord,
    they snatched a purple cloak,
your passion turned, for all they cared,
    into a soldier's joke.
They could not know, as we do now,
    that though we merit blame,
you will your robe of mercy throw
    around our naked shame.

3 A sceptered reed, O patient Lord,
    they thrust into your hand,
and acted out their grim charade
    to its appointed end.
They could not know, as we do now,
    though empires rise and fall,
your kingdom shall not cease to grow
    till love embraces all.

FRED PRATT GREEN (1903–2000)

turn to next page

HIS KINGLY RULE IN US

Reading: Praise (II)

King of Glorie, King of Peace,
    I will love thee:
And that love may never cease,
    I will move thee.

Thou hast granted my request,
    Thou hast heard me:
Thou didst note my working breast,
    Thou hast spar'd me.

Wherefore with my utmost art
    I will sing thee,
And the cream of all my heart
    I will bring thee.

Though my sinnes against me cried,
    Thou didst cleare me;
And alone, when they replied,
    Thou didst heare me.

Sev'n whole dayes, not one in seven,
    I will praise thee.
In my heart, though not in heaven,
    I can raise thee.

Thou grew'st soft and moist with tears,
    Thou relentedst:
And when Justice call'd for fears,
    Thou disentedst.

Small it is, in this poore sort
    To enroll thee:
Ev'n eternitie is to short
    To extoll thee.

GEORGE HERBERT (*from* THE TEMPLE, 1633)

Hymn

Alleluia, sing to Jesus (page 88)
      or
Crown him with many crowns (page 90)
      or
King of Kings, majesty (page 94)

Hymn: Alleluia, sing to Jesus

HYFRYDOL   87 87 D

Music: Melody by ROWLAND HUW PRICHARD (1811–1887)
           harmonised by Compilers of *English Hymnal*, 1906

1 Alleluia, sing to Jesus!
    his the sceptre, his the throne;
Alleluia, his the triumph,
    his the victory alone:
hark, the songs of peaceful Sion
    thunder like a mighty flood;
Jesus out of every nation
    hath redeemed us by his blood.

2 Alleluia, not as orphans
    are we left in sorrow now;
Alleluia, he is near us,
    faith believes, nor questions how:
though the cloud from sight received him,
    when the forty days were o'er,
shall our hearts forget his promise,
    'I am with you evermore'?

3 Alleluia, bread of angels,
    thou on earth our food, our stay;
Alleluia, here the sinful
    flee to thee from day to day:
Intercessor, Friend of sinners,
    earth's Redeemer, plead for me,
where the songs of all the sinless
    sweep across the crystal sea.

4 Alleluia, King eternal,
    thee the Lord of lords we own;
Alleluia, born of Mary,
    earth thy footstool, heaven thy throne:
thou within the veil hast entered,
    robed in flesh, our great High Priest;
thou on earth both Priest and Victim
    in the eucharistic feast.

WILLIAM CHATTERTON DIX (1837-1898)

turn to page 100

Hymn: Crown him with many crowns

DIADEMATA

DSM

1   Crown him with many crowns,
the Lamb upon his throne;
Hark! how the heavenly anthem drowns
all music but its own:
Awake, my soul, and sing
of him who died for thee,
and hail him as thy matchless King
through all eternity.

Music: GEORGE JOB ELVEY (1816–1893)
        last verse arrangement by ANDREW REID

2   Crown him the Virgin's Son,
      the God incarnate born,
whose arm those crimson trophies won
    which now his brow adorn:
    fruit of the mystic Rose,
    as of that Rose the Stem;
the Root whence mercy ever flows,
    the Babe of Bethlehem.

3   Crown him the Lord of Love!
    Behold his hands and side,
rich wounds yet visible above
    in beauty glorified:
    no angel in the sky
    can fully bear that sight,
but downward bends his burning eye
    at mysteries so bright.

4   Crown him the Lord of peace,
    whose power a sceptre sways
from pole to pole, that wars may cease,
    absorbed in prayer and praise:
    his reign shall know no end,
    and round his piercèd feet
fair flowers of Paradise extend
    their fragrance ever sweet.

turn over for last verse descant arrangement

5   Crown him the Lord of years,
    the Potentate of time,
Creator of the rolling spheres,
    ineffably sublime.
    Glassed in a sea of light,
    where everlasting waves
reflect his throne, the Infinite,
    who lives, and loves, and saves.

MATTHEW BRIDGES (1800-1894)

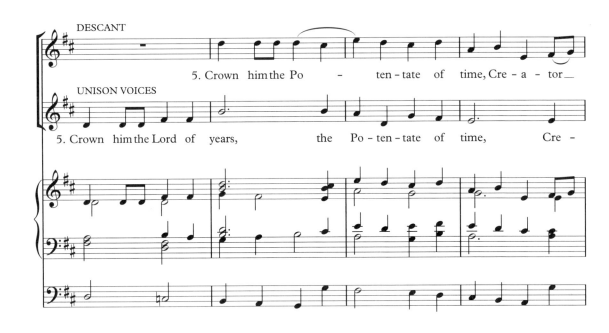

light, where e-ver-last-ing waves___ re-flect his throne, the

in a sea of light, where e-ver-last-ing waves re-

In-fi-nite, who lives, and loves, and saves.

-flect his throne, the In-fi-nite, who lives, and loves, and saves.

For Choral Evensong, turn to page 173

turn to page 100

Hymn: King of kings, majesty

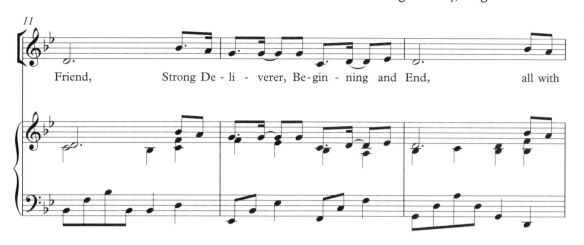

Friend, Strong De - li - verer, Be-gin - ning and End, all with

Refrain

-in me falls at your throne. Your ma - jes - ty, I can but

bow; I lay my all be-fore you now. In ro - yal

na - tions,   ran-somed souls,   brought this sin - ner_ near to_ your

throne:_____ all with - in   me   cries out_ in   praise._____ *Your ma -jes-*

-ty,_____ I can-not bow;_____ I lay my all_____ be-fore you

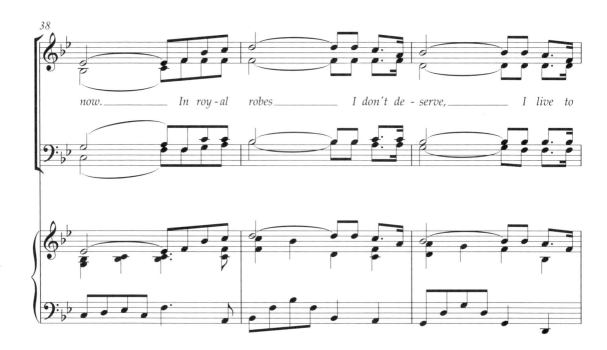

now._____ In roy-al robes_____ I don't de - serve,_____ I live to

Words and music: JARROD COOPER
arrangement by PAUL HUGHES

turn to next page

Homily/Address

THE KING OF GLORY

Anthem

Purcell: O God, the King of glory (see below)
or
Ireland: Te Deum in F (page 106)
or
Marenzio: O Rex gloriae (page 123)

Anthem: O God, the King of Glory

Words: Collect for the Sunday after Ascension Day

Music: Henry Purcell (1659–1695)
edited by Edward Tambling

gone   be - fore   us.   A - men.

___ is gone be - fore   us.   A - men.

gone   be - fore___   us.   A - men.

gone   be - fore   us.   A - men.

For Choral Evensong, turn to page 154

turn to page 128

Anthem: Te Deum laudamus

Words: ANCIENT HYMN OF THE CHURCH

Music: JOHN IRELAND
(1879–1962)

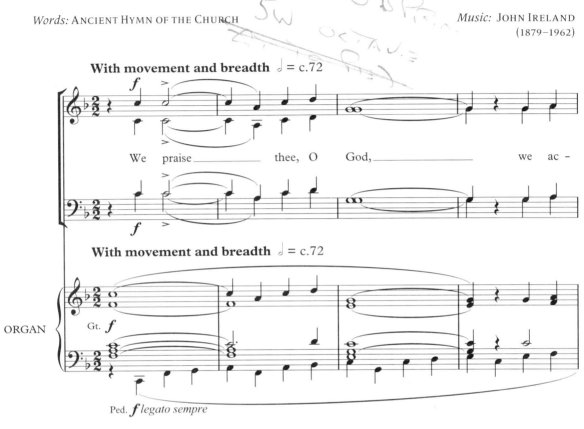

turn to page 128

Anthem: O Rex gloriae

Words: ANTIPHON TO THE MAGNIFICAT
for SECOND VESPERS AT ASCENSION

Music: LUCA MARENZIO
(1553–1599)
edited by EDWARD TAMBLING

Translation: O King of glory, Lord of all power,
Who ascended to heaven on this day triumphant over all;
Do not leave us as orphans, But send us the Father's promise,
The spirit of truth. Alleluia.

turn to next page

Presentation of Awards

Prayers

Let us pray

As we give thanks Lord for the privilege of this opportunity to worship
you as God and King so we pray for those who must worship in secret or
for fear of their lives.

All   Let all the world in every corner sing, my God and King!

Brief silence

As you invite us to fill the heavens with your praise so on earth may our
worship and service contribute to the growth in mission of your church
and kingdom.

All   The heavens are not too high, his praise may thither fly,
The earth is not too low, his praises there may grow.

Brief silence

As your kingship seeks to reach out in loving embrace of the whole
world, so may we make each church, each home, each community places
of welcome, places where hearts are touched and transformed.

All   The church with psalms must shout, no door can keep them out;
But, above all, the heart must bear the longest part.

Brief silence

When the heart is hard and parched up,
come upon me with a shower of mercy.
When grace is lost from life,
come with a burst of song.
When tumultuous work raises its din on all sides
shutting me out from beyond,
come to me, my Lord of silence,
with your peace and rest.
When my beggarly heart sits crouched,
shut up in a corner, break open the door, my king,
and come with the ceremony of a king.
When desire blinds the mind with delusion and dust,
O holy and wakeful One,
come with your light and your thunder.

RABINDRANATH TAGORE
adapted from *God of a Hundred Names*,
BARBARA GREENE and VICTOR GOLLANCZ (1962, *p.* 204)

All   **Let all the world in every corner sing, my God and King!**

So let us pray for the coming of the kingdom in its fullness, as our
Saviour has taught us:

All   **Our Father, who art in heaven,**
hallowed be thy name;
thy kingdom come;
thy will be done;
on earth as it is in heaven.
Give us this day our daily bread.
And forgive us our trespasses,
as we forgive those who trespass against us.
And lead us not into temptation;
but deliver us from evil.
For thine is the kingdom,
the power and the glory,
for ever and ever.
Amen.

Anthem

Philip Duffy: A Song of Salvation (see below)
or
Bairstow: Let all mortal flesh (page 134)
or
Rachmaninoff: The Cherubic Hymn (page 143)

Philip Duffy: A Song of Salvation

Words: from REVELATION 19

Music: PHILIP DUFFY
(*b.*1934)

* This antiphon may be sung by choir and then by the choir and ALL at the start.

© Philip Duffy. Used with permission.

turn to page 153

Anthem: Let all mortal flesh keep silence

Words from The Liturgy of St James

Music: Edward C. Bairstow
(1874-1946)

* *If found too high for male altos, these notes may be omitted, or the Introit may be sung in F minor.*

This edition © 2017 The Royal School of Church Music.

For Choral Evensong, turn to page 154

turn to page 153

Anthem: The Cherubic Hymn

Words: from THE LITURGY OF ST JOHN CHRYSOSTOM

Music: SERGEI RACHMANINOFF
(1873–1943)

al — le — lu — — — ia.
a — lee — lui — — — ya.

— — ia, al — le — lu — ia.
— ya, a — lee — lui — ya.

-lu — — — — ia.
-lui — — — — ya.

— — — — ia.
— — — — ya.

continue to next page

Blessing

Christ our King make you faithful and strong to do his will,
that you may reign with him in glory;
and the blessing of God Almighty,
the Father, the Son, and the Holy Spirit,
be among you and remain with you always.

All   **Amen.**

Recessional Hymn

Rejoice the Lord is King (page 154)
or
You're the word of God the Father (page 160)

Hymn: Rejoice the Lord is King

Music: Melody and bass by GEORGE FREDERICK HANDEL (1685–1759)
          arranged by ANDREW REID

- joice.

4. He sits at God's right hand   till

all his _ foes sub-mit,   and bow to his com-mand,   and fall be-neath his feet:

lift up your heart, lift up your voice; re-joice, a-gain, I __ say, re-

Man.   Ped.

-joice.

UNISON

5. Re - joice in glo - rious

hope;   Je - sus   the__ Judge   shall come,   and

CHARLES WESLEY (1707–1788)

Hymn: You're the Word of God the Father (Across the lands)

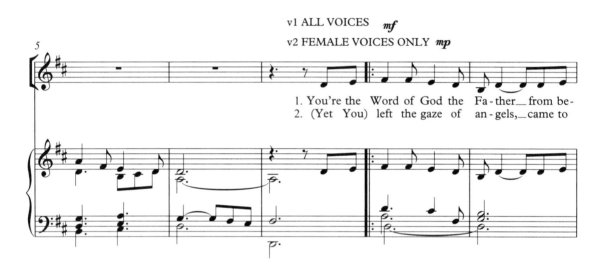

v1 ALL VOICES *mf*
v2 FEMALE VOICES ONLY *mp*

1. You're the Word of God the Fa-ther__ from be-
2. (Yet You) left the gaze of an-gels,__ came to

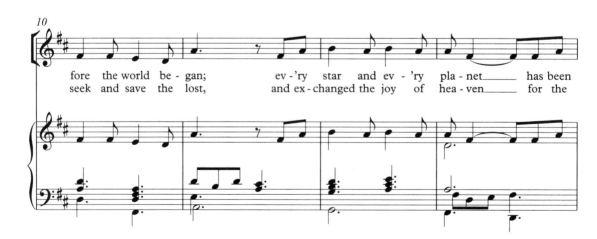

fore the world be-gan;   ev-'ry star and ev-'ry pla-net__ has been
seek and save the lost,   and ex-changed the joy of hea-ven__ for the

Words and Music: © 2002 Thankyou Music / admin by CapitolCMGPublishing.com excl. UK & Europe, admin by
Integrity Music, part of the David C Cook family songs@integritymusic.com Used by permission

Words and Music: KEITH GETTY and STUART TOWNEND
arrangement by PAUL HUGHES

Additional
Choral Resources

Preces and Responses for Unison Voices

Words: THE BOOK OF COMMON PRAYER   *Music:* HARRY BRAMMA

The Preces

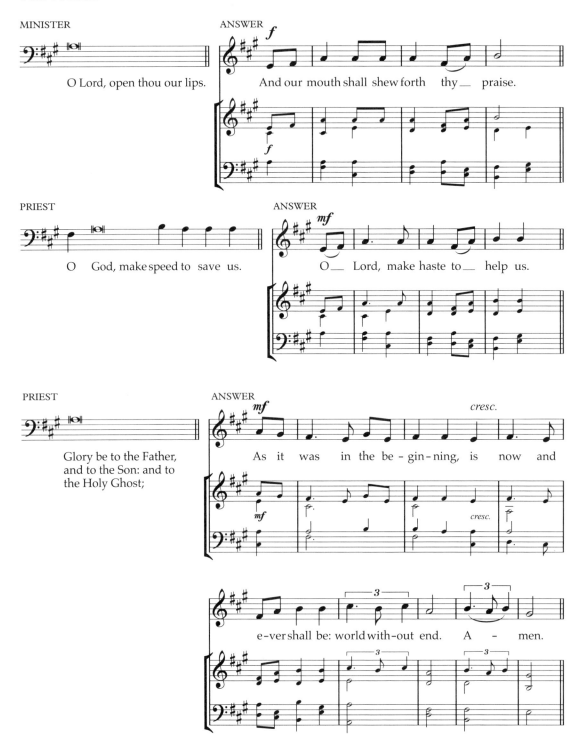

MINISTER
O Lord, open thou our lips.

ANSWER *f*
And our mouth shall shew forth thy praise.

PRIEST
O God, make speed to save us.

ANSWER *mf*
O Lord, make haste to help us.

PRIEST
Glory be to the Father, and to the Son: and to the Holy Ghost;

ANSWER *mf* *cresc.*
As it was in the be-gin-ning, is now and e-ver shall be: world with-out end. A - men.

PRIEST
Praise ye the Lord.

ANSWER
The Lord's Name be prais'd.

For Choral Evensong, turn to page 32

The Apostles' Creed

I BELIEVE in God the Father Almighty,
Maker of heaven and earth:
And in Jesus Christ his only Son our Lord,
Who was conceived by the Holy Ghost,
Born of the Virgin Mary,
Suffered under Pontius Pilate,
Was crucified, dead, and buried:
He descended into hell;
The third day he rose again from the dead;
He ascended into heaven,
And sitteth on the right hand of God the Father Almighty;
From thence he shall come to judge the quick and the dead.
I believe in the Holy Ghost;
The holy Catholick Church;
The Communion of Saints;
The Forgiveness of sins;
The Resurrection of the body,
And the Life everlasting.
Amen.

The Responses

The Lord's Prayer

PRIEST

ANSWER

O Lord, shew thy mercy up-on us.

And grant us __ thy sal - va - tion.

PRIEST

ANSWER

O Lord, save the Queen.

And mer-ci - ful -ly __ hear us   when we call up-on thee.

PRIEST

ANSWER

Endue thy ministers
with right-eous-ness.

And make thy __ cho-sen __ peo-ple   joy - ful.

PRIEST

ANSWER

O Lord, save thy peo - ple.

And bless _____ thine in - he - ri-tance.

THE COLLECTS

For Choral Evensong, turn to page 100 or 134

Magnificat & Nunc dimittis
Salisbury Festival Service

Magnificat

Words: from LUKE 1. 47–55
THE BOOK OF COMMON PRAYER

Music: GRAYSTON IVES

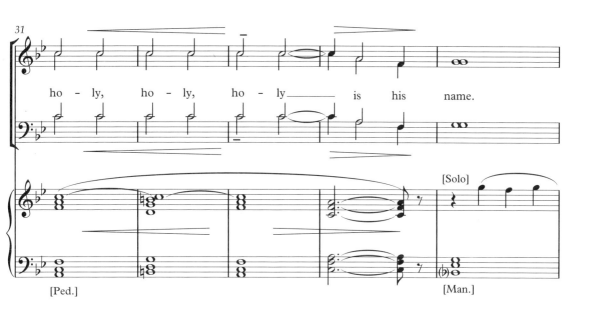

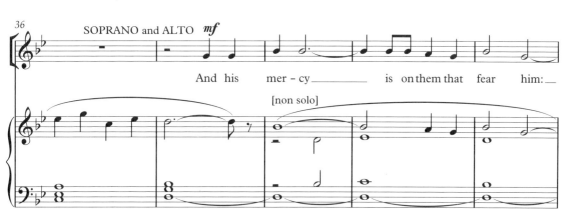

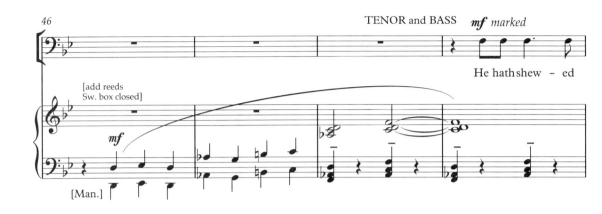

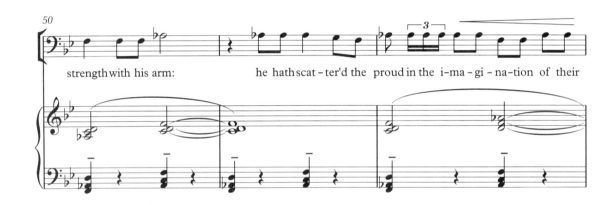

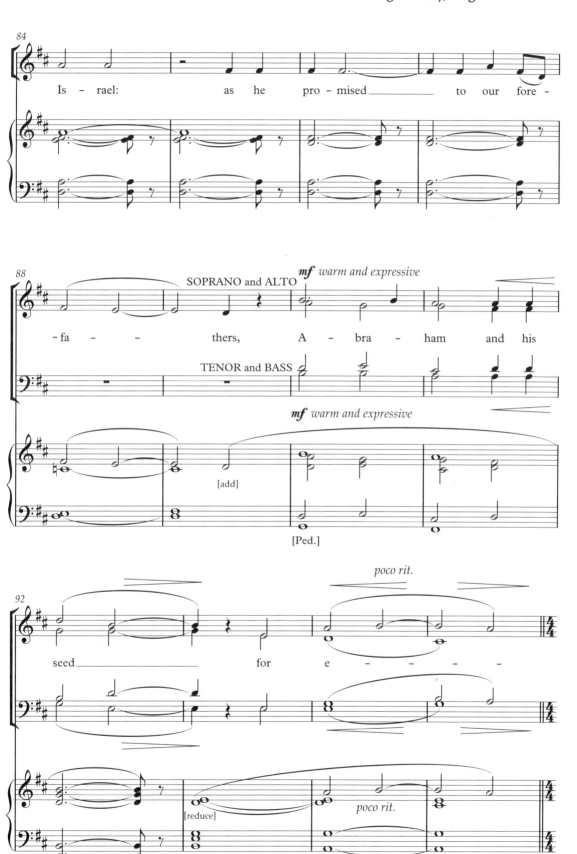

GLORIA

Nunc dimittis

Words: from LUKE 2. 29–32
The Book of Common Prayer

Music: GRAYSTON IVES

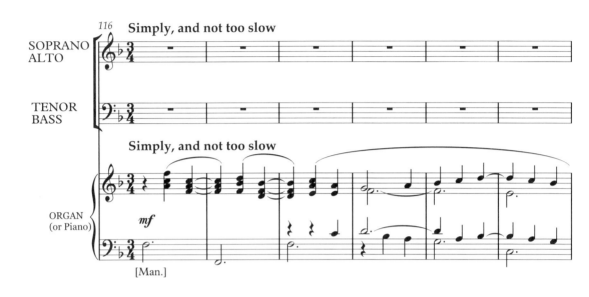

GLORIA

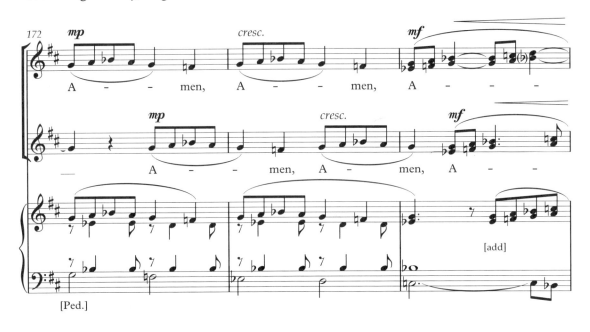

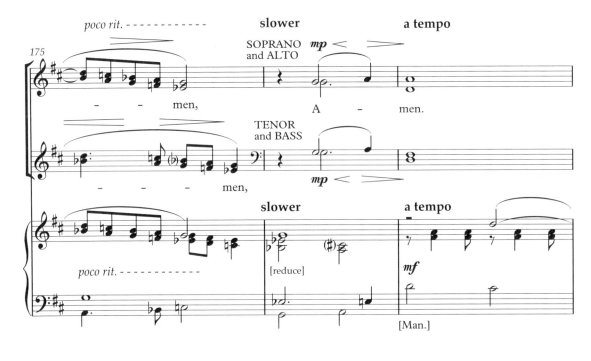

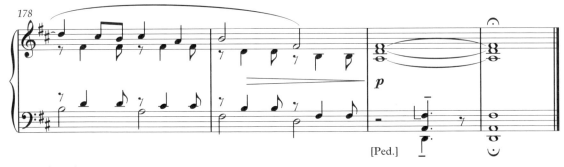

For Choral Evensong, turn to page 167